Carom Billiards: Around the World Patterns

3-Cushion Billiards Championship Shots

From International Competitions

(Test Yourself against Professional Players)

Allan P. Sand
PBIA Certified Instructor

ISBN 978-1-62505-222-3
PRINT 7x11

ISBN 978-1-62505-416-6
PRINT 8.5x11

First edition

Copyright © 2016 Allan P. Sand

All rights reserved under International and Pan-American Copyright Conventions.

Published by Billiard Gods Productions.
Santa Clara, CA 95051
U.S.A.

For the latest information about books and videos, go to: http://www.billiardgods.com

Acknowledgements

Wei Chao created the software that was used to create these graphics.

Table of Contents

Introduction 1
About the Graphic Layouts 1
Table Setup 2
Purpose of the Layouts 2
A: Short Leg into Long Rail 3
A: Group 1 3
A: Group 2 8
A: Group 3 13
A: Group 4 18
A: Group 5 23
A: Group 6 28
A: Group 7 33
B: Reverse Patterns 38
B: Group 1 38
B: Group 2 43
B: Group 3 48
B: Group 4 53
C: Extended Patterns 58
C: Group 1 58
C: Group 2 63
C: Group 3 68
D: Big Ball in the Home Corner 73
D: Group 1 73
D: Group 2 78
D: Group 3 83
D: Group 4 88
D: Group 5 93
D: Group 6 98
D: Group 7 103
D: Group 8 108
D: Group 9 113
E: Follow into the Corner Pattern 118
E: Group 1 118
E: Group 2 123
E: Group 3 128
F: Short Modified Pattern 133
F: Group 1 133
F: Group 2 138

Other books by the author ...

- 3 Cushion Billiards Championship Shots (a series)
- Carom Billiards: Some Riddles & Puzzles
- Carom Billiards: MORE Riddles & Puzzles
- Why Pool Hustlers Win
- Table Map Library
- Safety Toolbox
- Cue Ball Control Cheat Sheets
- Advanced Cue Ball Control Self-Testing Program
- Drills & Exercises for Pool & Pocket Billiards
- The Art of War versus The Art of Pool
- The Psychology of Losing – Tricks, Traps & Sharks
- The Art of Team Coaching
- The Art of Personal Competition
- The Art of Politics & Campaigning
- The Art of Marketing & Promotion
- Kitchen God's Guide for Single Guys

Introduction

This is one of a series of Carom Billiards books that show how professional players select shots, based on the table layout. All of these shots have been mapped out based on shots played at international competitions.

This book contains a wide variety of examples of the CB paths known as "around the world" patterns.

These shots put you inside the head of the player beginning with the ball positions (shown in the first table layout). The second table layout shows the shooting decision and the results of the player's choice.

About the Graphic Layouts

There are two graphics for each shot. The first graphic shows the ball positions on the table. The ball labeled "A" is always the player's CB. The first graphic the ball positions on the table. The second graphic shows how the shot was played.

Each table graphic in this book is a black & white representation of a standard 5 x 10 carom billiards table. Balls are represented with these three symbols.

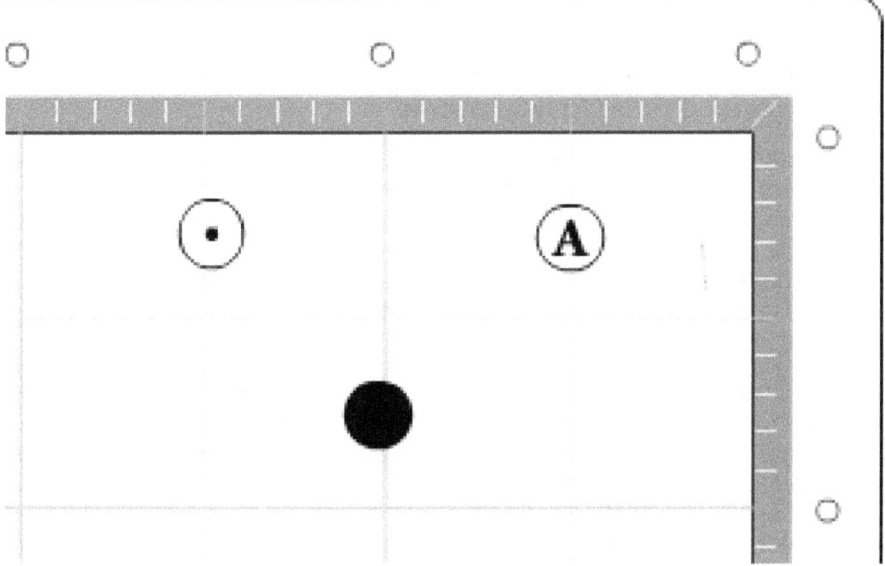

(A) The white "A" ball "A" is ALWAYS the shooter's cue ball.

(·) The white "center dot" ball is always the opponent's cue ball.

● This is the red Object Ball, represented in the layouts as the black ball.

Each shot is represented with two layouts on each page. The first layout shows the ball position setup BEFORE the shot. The second layout shows the ball pathways that the balls travel during the shot.

Table Setup

1. Use donuts (paper reinforcement rings) to mark positions for the carom balls. These are available at any office supply store.

2. Place chalk cubes at the locations where the CB contacts each rail.

When you play the shot, observe where the CB pattern and each rail contact. You may need several attempts as you make adjustments to the CB spin to properly follow the pattern.

Purpose of the Layouts

These are examples of shots that champion 3-cushion players from all over the world had to play. The first graphic provides the layout. The second graphic provides the results of their shooting solution. These layouts are provided for two purposes.

- Use the first layout as a mental exercise. The player picked one, but there are many possibilities. From the comfort of your armchair, you can consider multiple options, and work out the pattern using the spin and speed you would have applied. These help stretch and extend your skills in tactical analysis. Then consider how the player decided how to shoot the shot. From the patterns you can determine how the CB was played and the type of applied spin. It's helpful to use a pointer (or your finger) to trace the pattern as you work out how the shot was played.

- The second purpose is to take these layouts to the practice table. Position the paper reinforcement rings in place for each ball. You are going to shoot the layout many times, so these donuts help mark the ball positions for each attempt. BEFORE you experiment with your own "solutions", shoot the pattern until you can easily duplicate the paths. This means you will do a lot of experimentation to find the spin/speed used by the original player. Only AFTER you understand and can execute the pattern should you experiment with your own ideas.

This combination of mental analysis and practical table practice will boost your growth as an intelligent and thinking carom billiards player.

A: Short Leg into Long Rail

On this series of shots, the CB goes into the first OB, which is very close to the cushion. The CB then goes into the standard "around the world" pattern. This sends the CB into the Home corner path.

A: Group 1

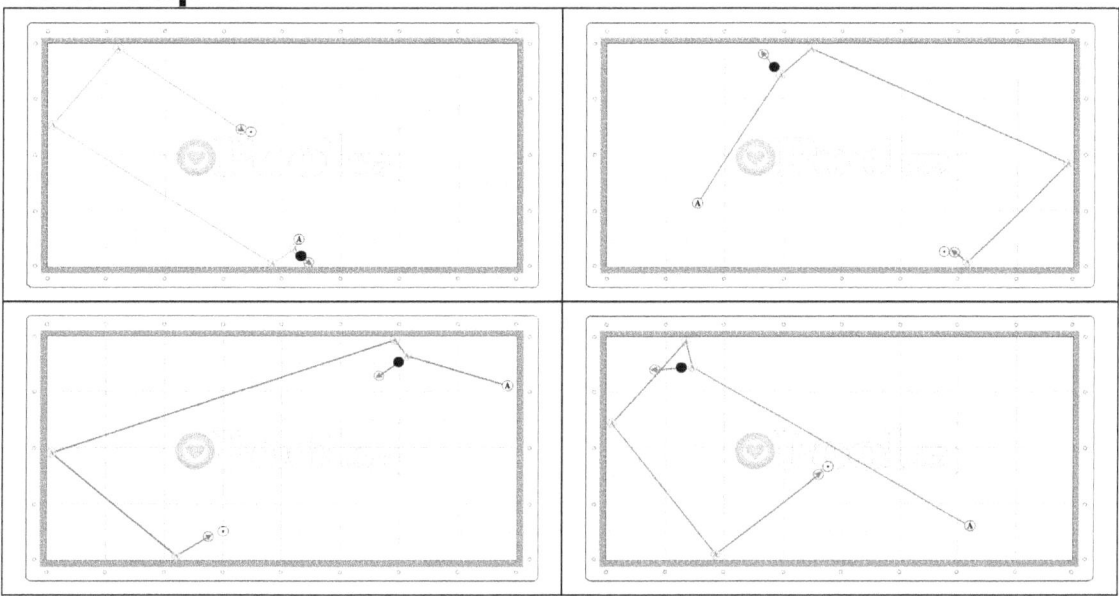

Analysis:

A:1a. _____

A:1b. _____

A:1c. _____

A:1d. _____

A:1a – Setup

Shot Pattern

A:1b – Setup

Shot Pattern

A:1c – Setup

Shot Pattern

A:1d – Setup

Shot Pattern

A: Group 2

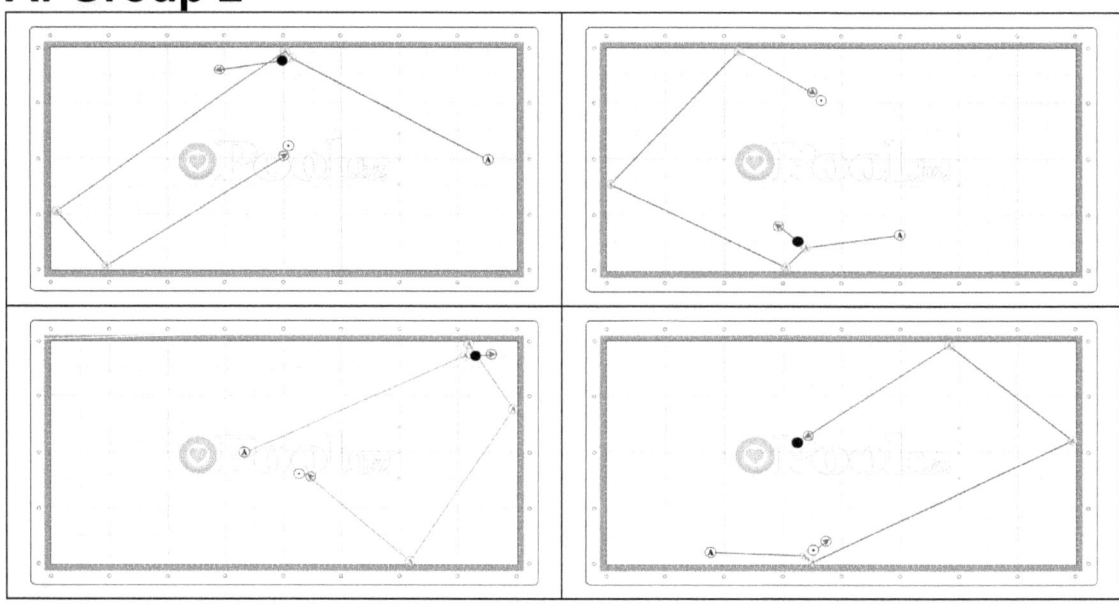

Analysis:

A:2a. _____

A:2b. _____

A:2c. _____

A:2d. _____

A:2a – Setup

Shot Pattern

A:2b – Setup

Shot Pattern

A:2c – Setup

Shot Pattern

A:2d – Setup

Shot Pattern

A: Group 3

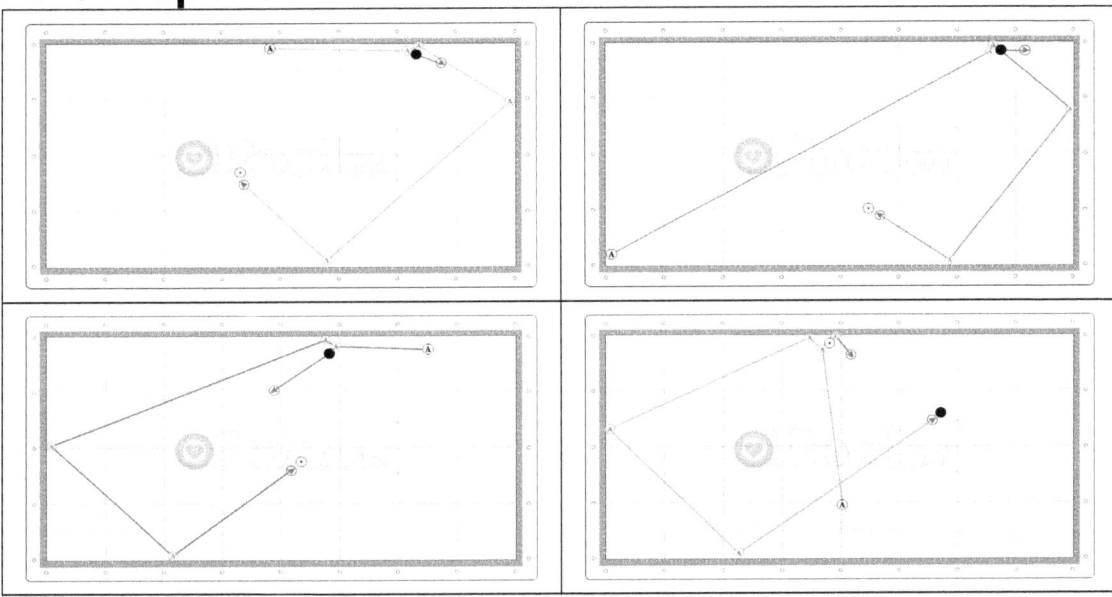

Analysis:

A:3a. _____

A:3b. _____

A:3c. _____

A:3d. _____

A:3a – Setup

Shot Pattern

A:3b – Setup

Shot Pattern

A:3c – Setup

Shot Pattern

A:3d – Setup

Shot Pattern

A: Group 4

Analysis:

A:4a. _____

A:4b. _____

A:4c. _____

A:4d. _____

A:4a – Setup

Shot Pattern

A:4b – Setup

Shot Pattern

A:4c – Setup

Shot Pattern

A:4d – Setup

Shot Pattern

A: Group 5

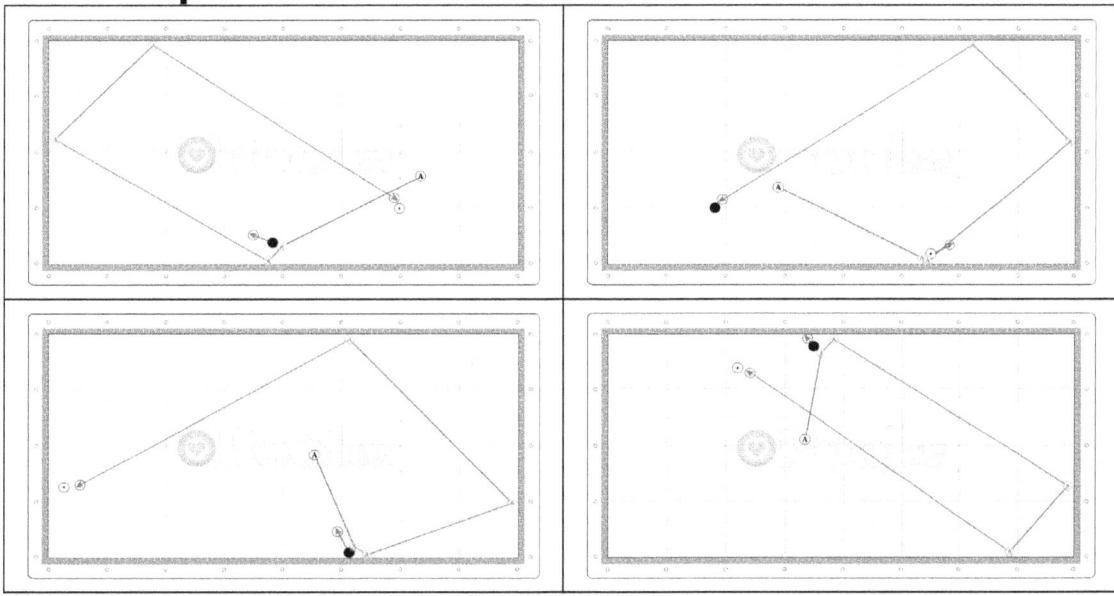

Analysis:

A:5a. _____

A:5b. _____

A:5c. _____

A:5d. _____

A:5a – Setup

Shot Pattern

A:5b – Setup

Shot Pattern

A:5c – Setup

Shot Pattern

A:5d – Setup

Shot Pattern

A: Group 6

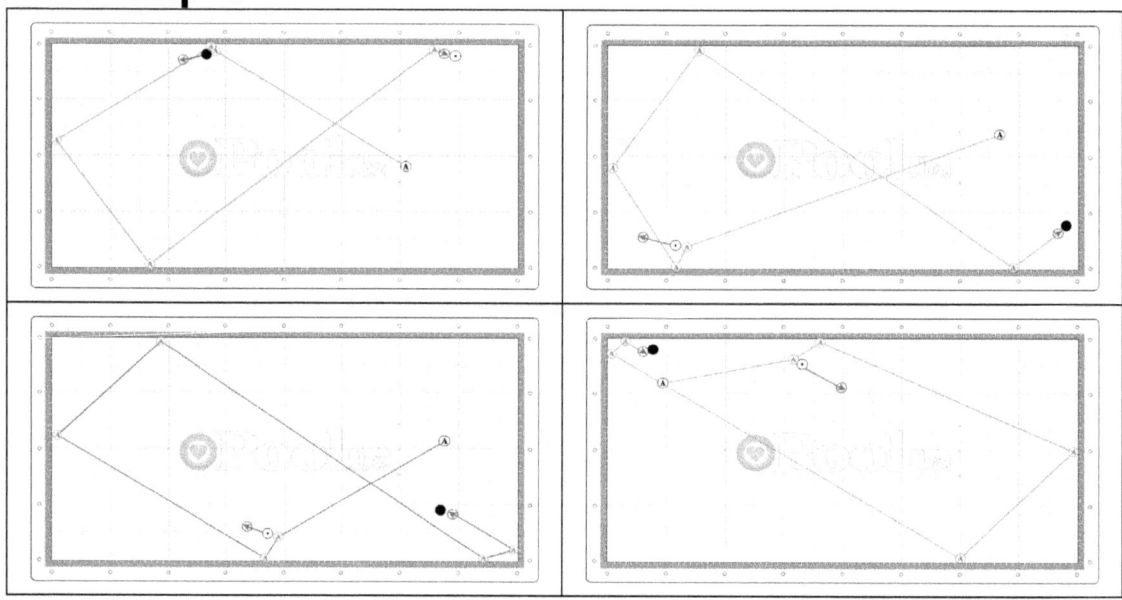

Analysis:

A:6a. _____

A:6b. _____

A:6c. _____

A:6d. _____

A:6a – Setup

Shot Pattern

A:6b – Setup

Shot Pattern

A:6c – Setup

Shot Pattern

A:6d – Setup

Shot Pattern

A: Group 7

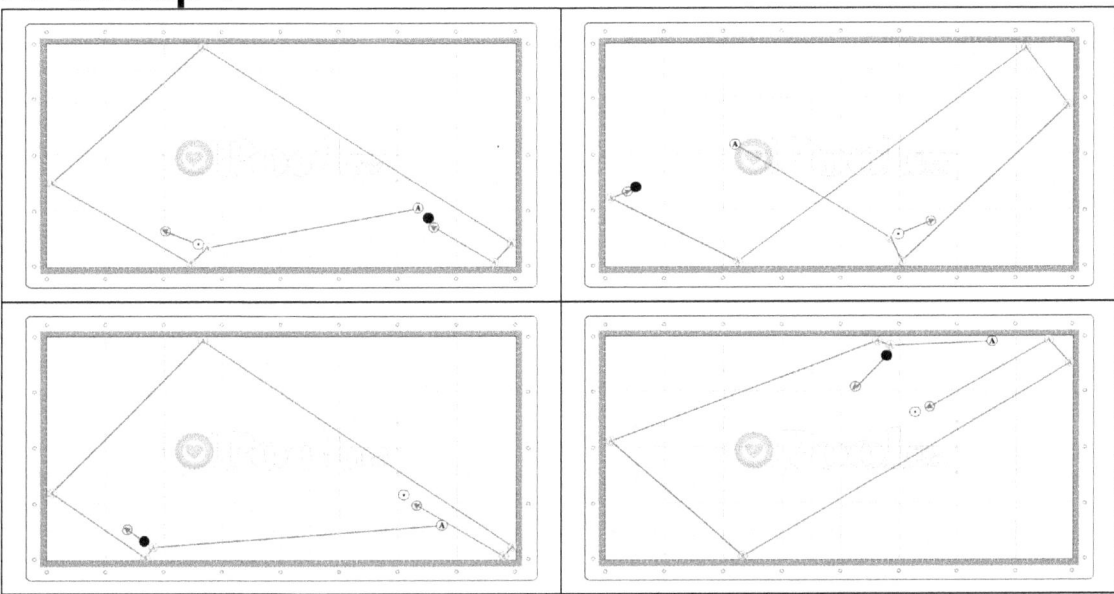

Analysis:

A:7a. _____

A:7b. _____

A:7c. _____

A:7d. _____

A:7a – Setup

Shot Pattern

A:7b – Setup

Shot Pattern

A:7c – Setup

Shot Pattern

A:7d – Setup

Shot Pattern

B: Reverse Patterns

On this set of successful shots, the CB goes into the first OB with some applied draw and side spin. This sends the CB back from the tangent line in a reverse pattern. The CB follows the standard around the world pattern towards the Home corner.

B: Group 1

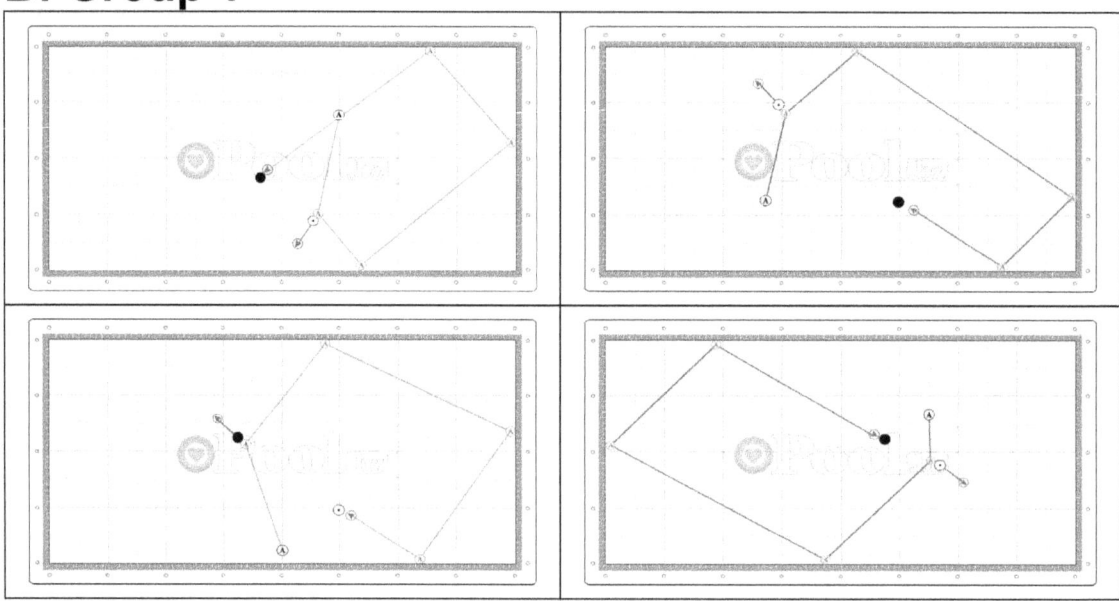

Analysis:

B:1a. _____

B:1b. _____

B:1c. _____

B:1d. _____

B:1a – Setup

Shot Pattern

B:1b – Setup

Shot Pattern

B:1c – Setup

Shot Pattern

B:1d – Setup

Shot Pattern

B: Group 2

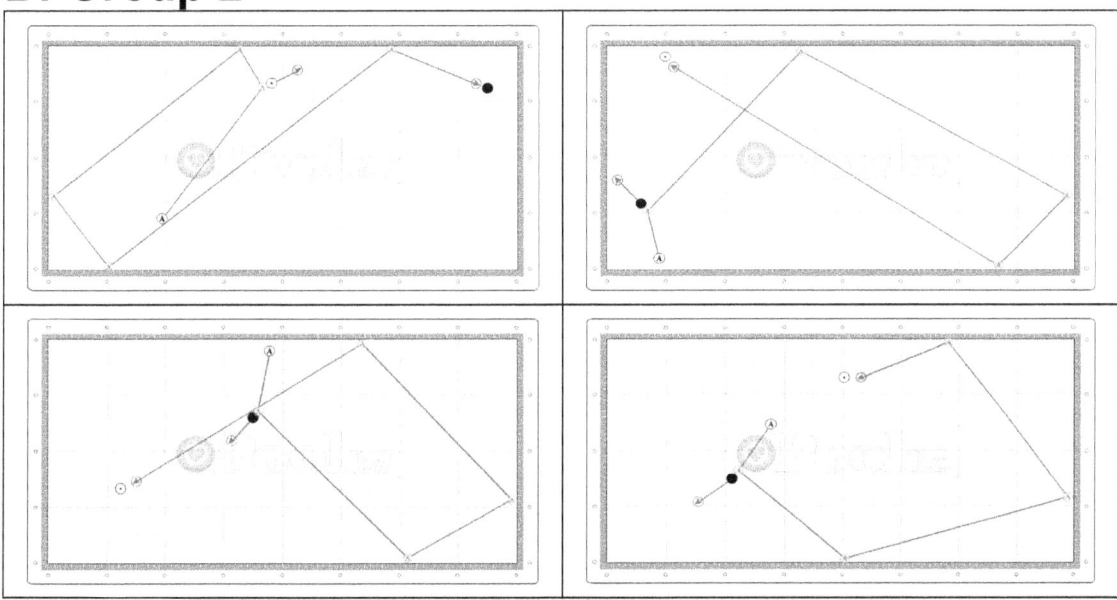

Analysis:

B:2a. _____

B:2b. _____

B:2c. _____

B:2d. _____

B:2a – Setup

Shot Pattern

B:2b – Setup

Shot Pattern

B:2c – Setup

Shot Pattern

B:2d – Setup

Shot Pattern

B: Group 3

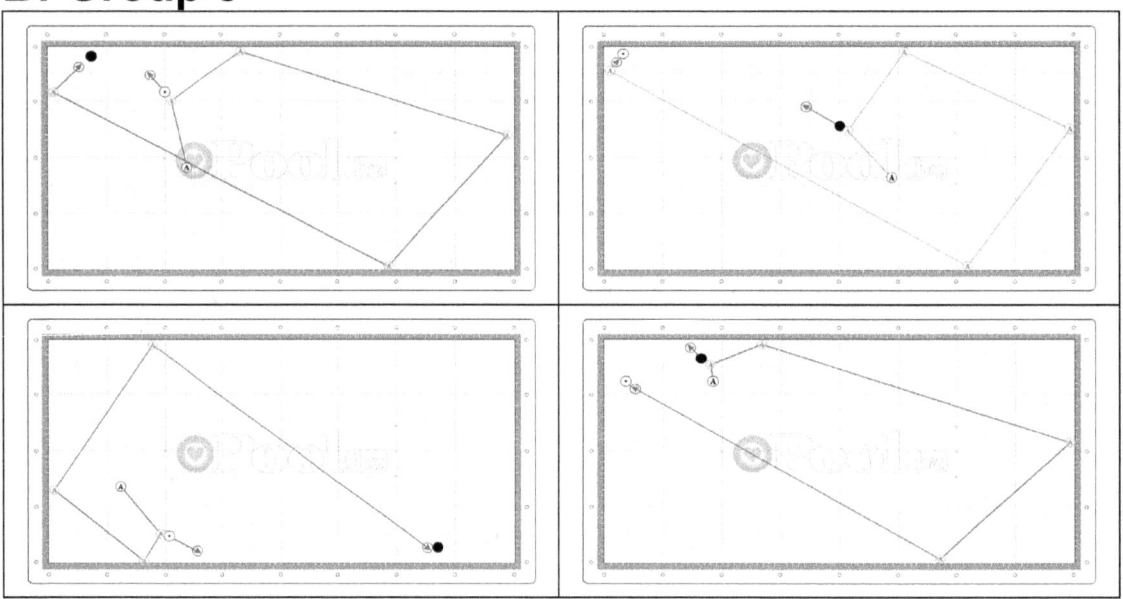

Analysis:

B:3a. _____

B:3b. _____

B:3c. _____

B:3d. _____

B:3a – Setup

Shot Pattern

B:3b – Setup

Shot Pattern

B:3c – Setup

Shot Pattern

B:3d – Setup

Shot Pattern

B: Group 4

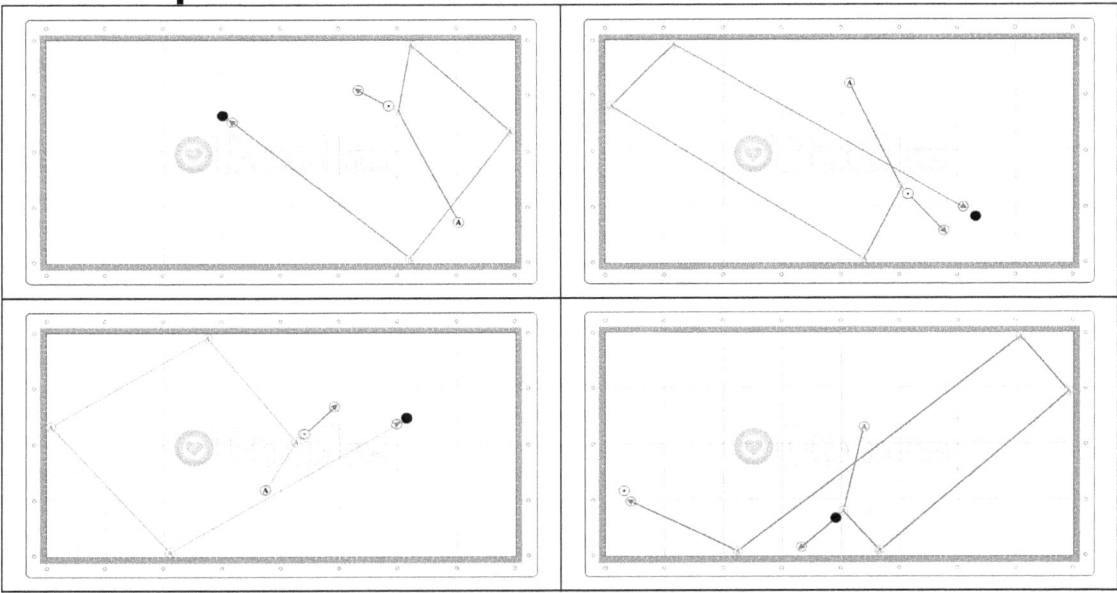

Analysis:

B:4a. _____

B:4b. _____

B:4c. _____

B:4d. _____

B:4a – Setup

Shot Pattern

B:4b – Setup

Shot Pattern

B:4c – Setup

Shot Pattern

B:4d – Setup

Shot Pattern

C: Extended Patterns

On these shots the CB contacts the first OB and starts the standard around the world pattern. The CB goes into the Home corner. Then it comes two rails out of the Home corner and travels into the second OB.

C: Group 1

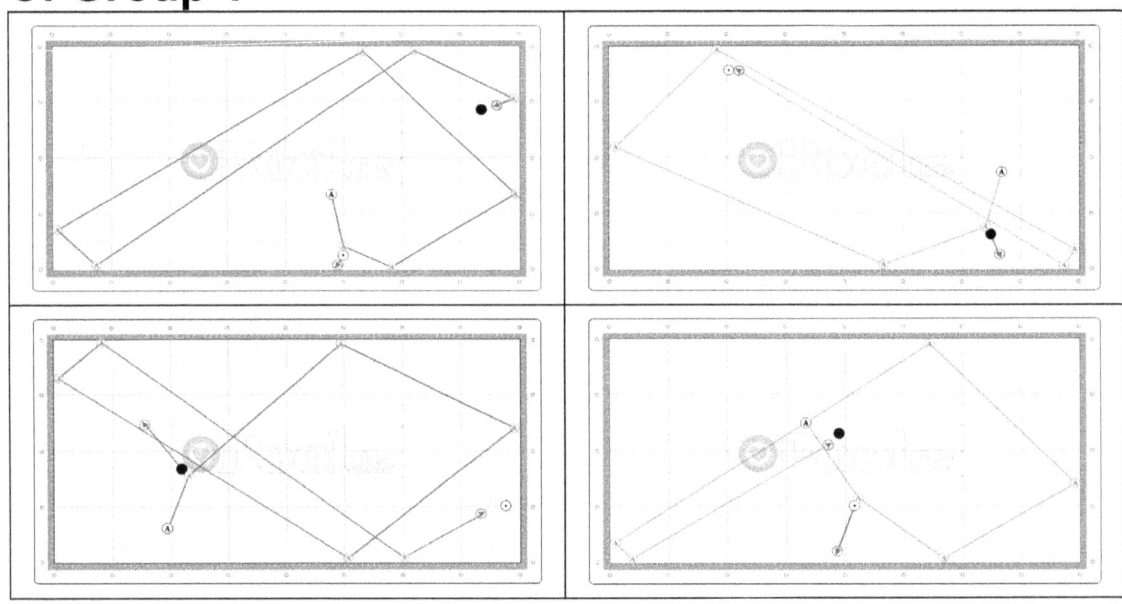

Analysis:

C:1a. _____

C:1b. _____

C:1c. _____

C:1d. _____

C:1a – Setup

Shot Pattern

C:1b – Setup

Shot Pattern

C:1c – Setup

Shot Pattern

C:1d – Setup

Shot Pattern

C: Group 2

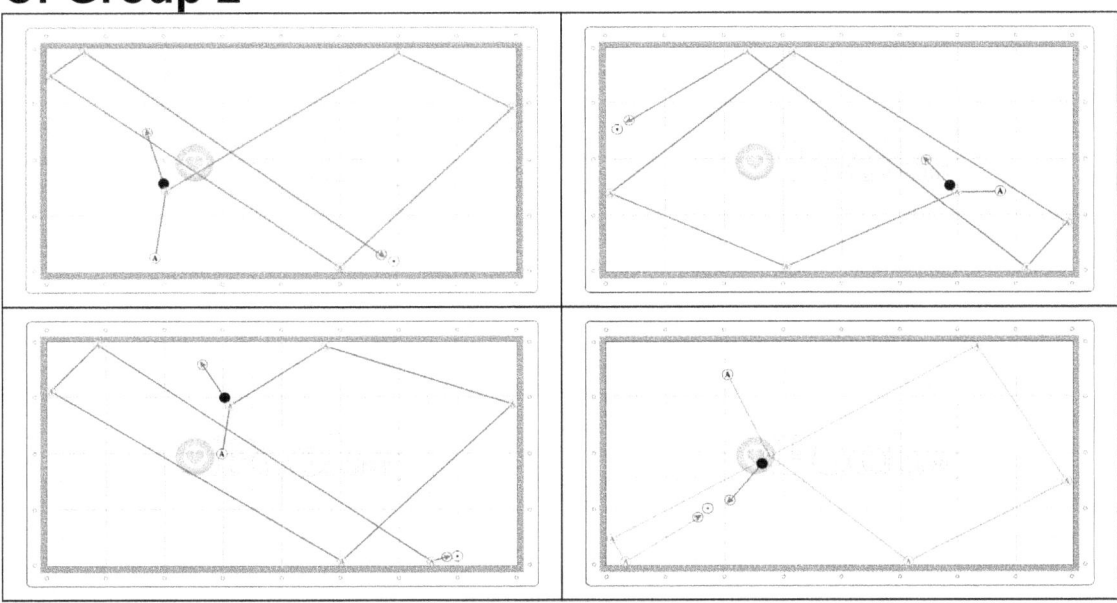

Analysis:

C:2a. _____

C:2b. _____

C:2c. _____

C:2d. _____

C:2a – Setup

Shot Pattern

C:2b – Setup

Shot Pattern

C:2c – Setup

Shot Pattern

C:2d – Setup

Shot Pattern

C: Group 3

Analysis:

C:3a. _____

C:3b. _____

C:3c. _____

C:3d. _____

C:3a – Setup

Shot Pattern

C:3b – Setup

Shot Pattern

C:3c – Setup

Shot Pattern

C:3d – Setup

Shot Pattern

D: Big Ball in the Home Corner

The CB comes off the first OB and follows the basic "Around the World" pattern. Because the second OB is in the corner, the target OB is "larger". Several of these shots show how the CB can go into the Home corner off one or both rails and hit the second OB for the score.

D: Group 1

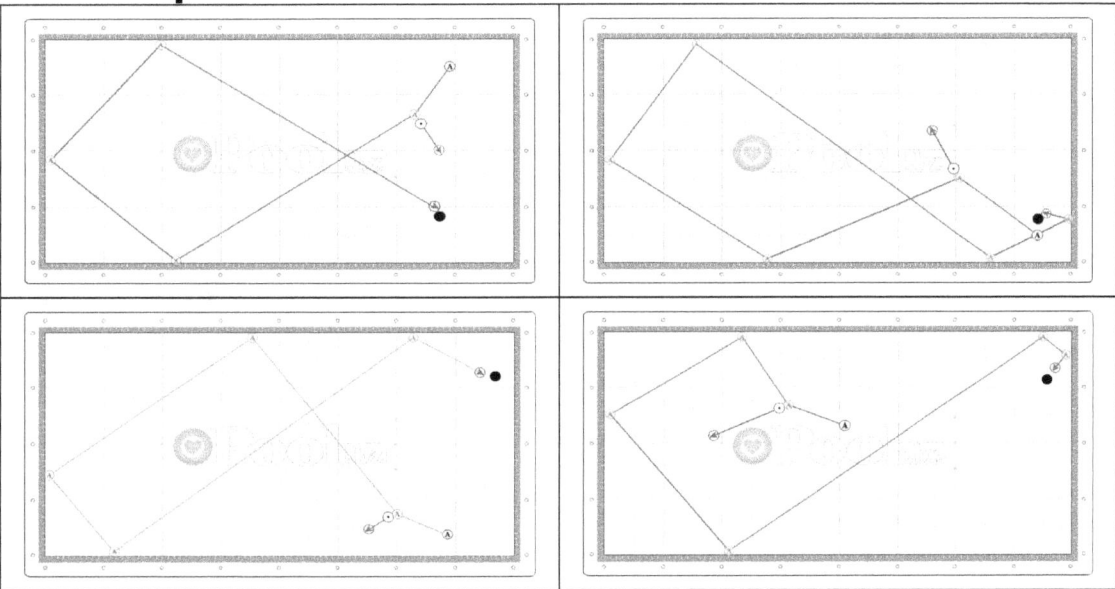

Analysis:

D:1a. _____

D:1b. _____

D:1c. _____

D:1d. _____

D:1a – Setup

Shot Pattern

D:1b – Setup

Shot Pattern

D:1c – Setup

Shot Pattern

D:1d – Setup

Shot Pattern

D: Group 2

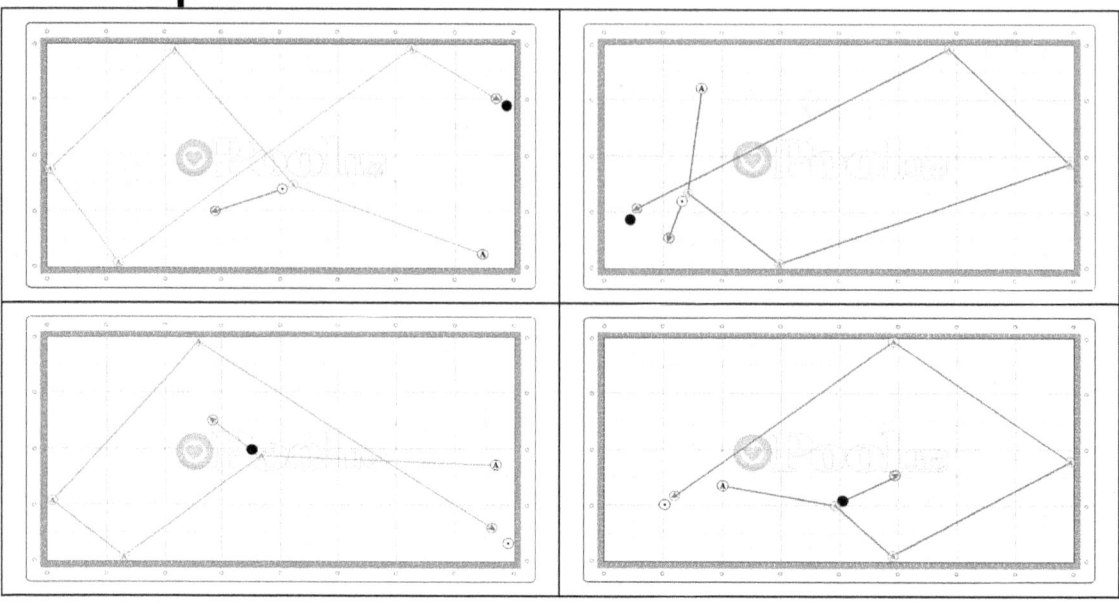

Analysis:

D:2a. _____

D:2b. _____

D:2c. _____

D:2d. _____

D:2a – Setup

Shot Pattern

D:2b – Setup

Shot Pattern

D:2c – Setup

Shot Pattern

D:2d – Setup

Shot Pattern

D: Group 3

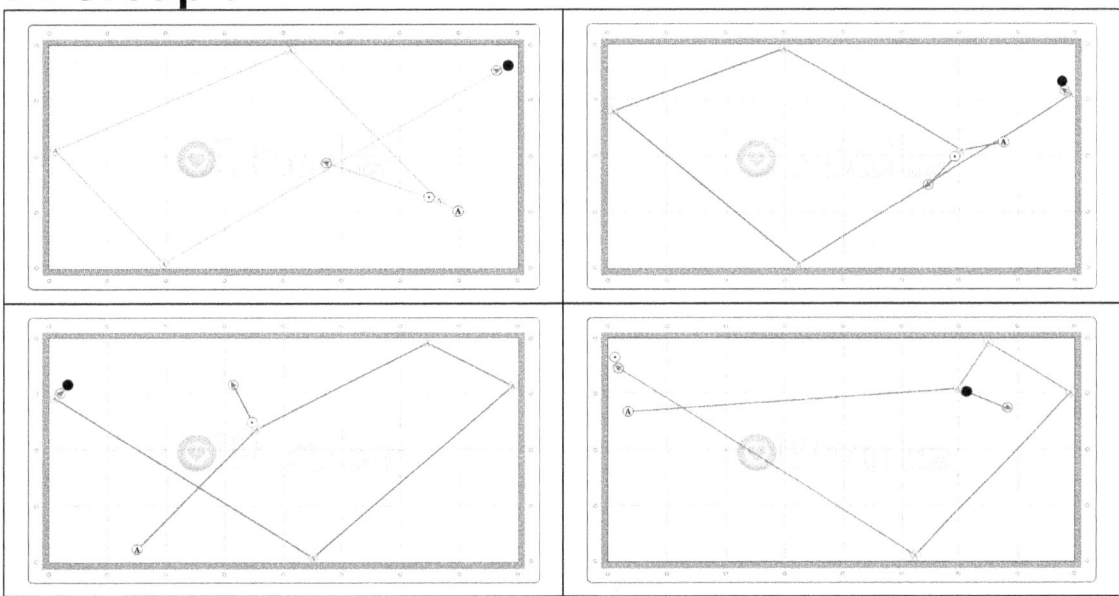

Analysis:

D:3a. _____

D:3b. _____

D:3c. _____

D:3d. _____

D:3a – Setup

Shot Pattern

D:3b – Setup

Shot Pattern

D:3c – Setup

Shot Pattern

D:3d – Setup

Shot Pattern

D: Group 4

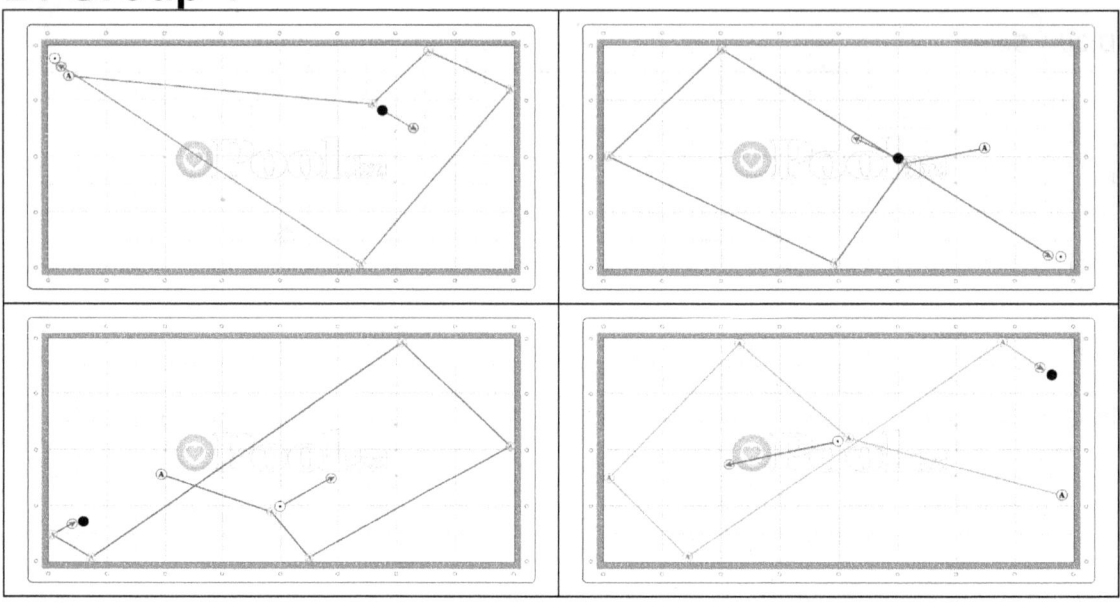

Analysis:

D:4a. _____

D:4b. _____

D:4c. _____

D:4d. _____

D:4a – Setup

Shot Pattern

D:4b – Setup

Shot Pattern

D:4c – Setup

Shot Pattern

D:4d – Setup

Shot Pattern

D: Group 5

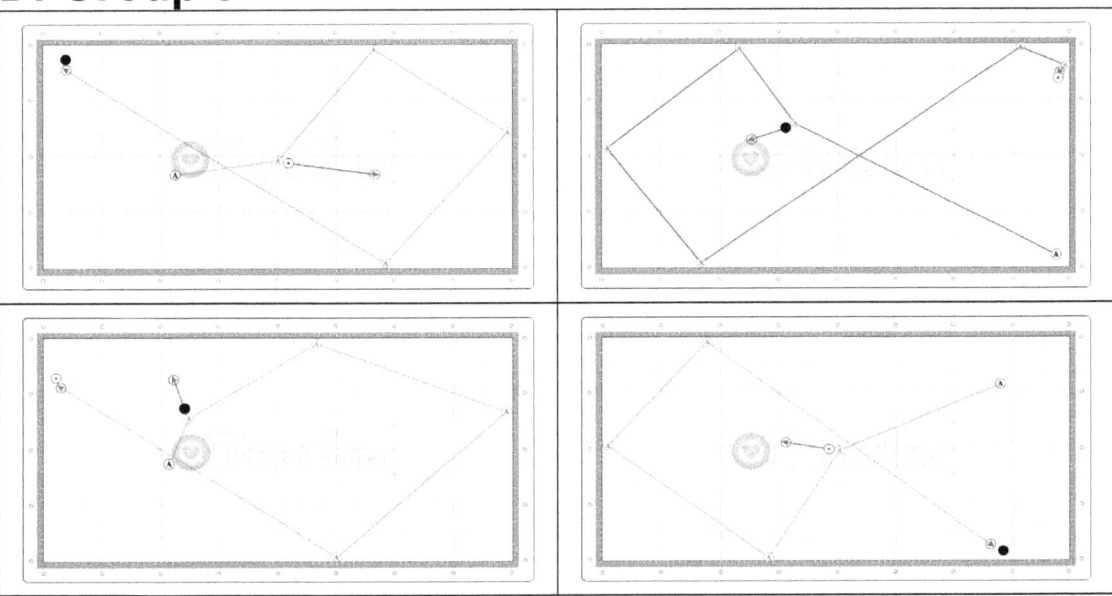

Analysis:

D:5a. _____

D:5b. _____

D:5c. _____

D:5d. _____

D:5a – Setup

Shot Pattern

D:5b – Setup

Shot Pattern

D:5c – Setup

Shot Pattern

D:5d – Setup

Shot Pattern

D: Group 6

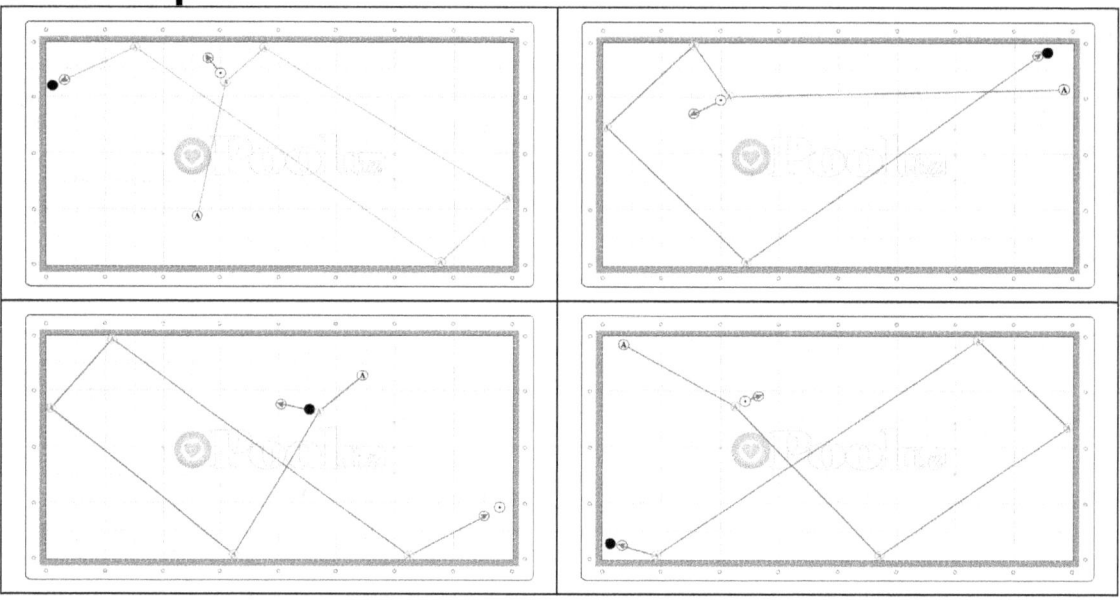

Analysis:

D:6a. _____

D:6b. _____

D:6c. _____

D:6d. _____

D:6a – Setup

Shot Pattern

D:6b – Setup

Shot Pattern

D:6c – Setup

Shot Pattern

D:6d – Setup

Shot Pattern

D: Group 7

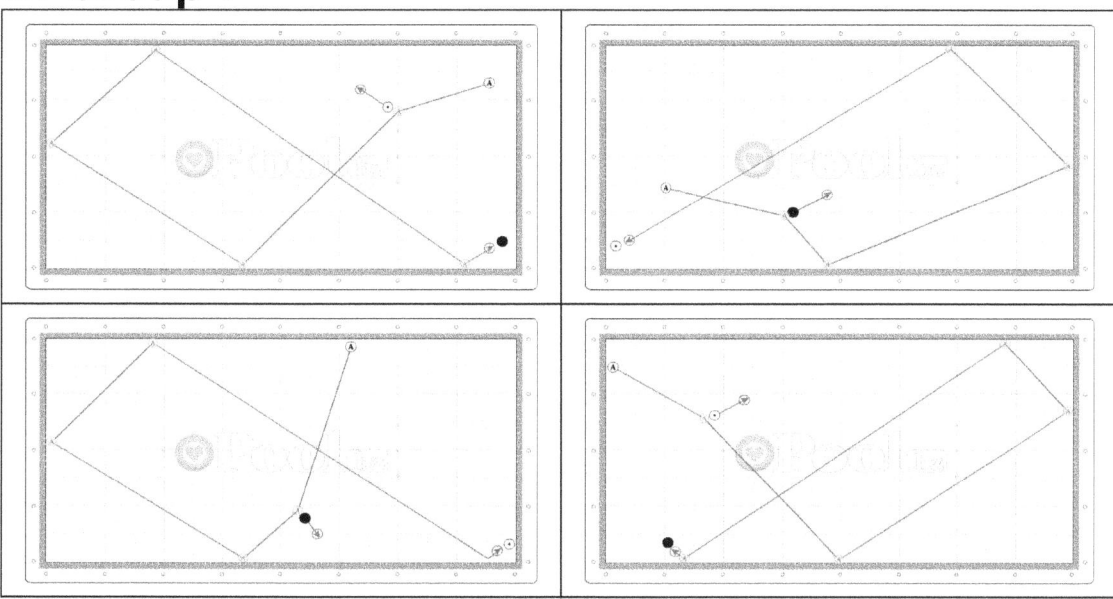

Analysis:

D:7a. _____

D:7b. _____

D:7c. _____

D:7d. _____

D:7a – Setup

Shot Pattern

D:7b – Setup

Shot Pattern

D:7c – Setup

Shot Pattern

D:7d – Setup

Shot Pattern

D: Group 8

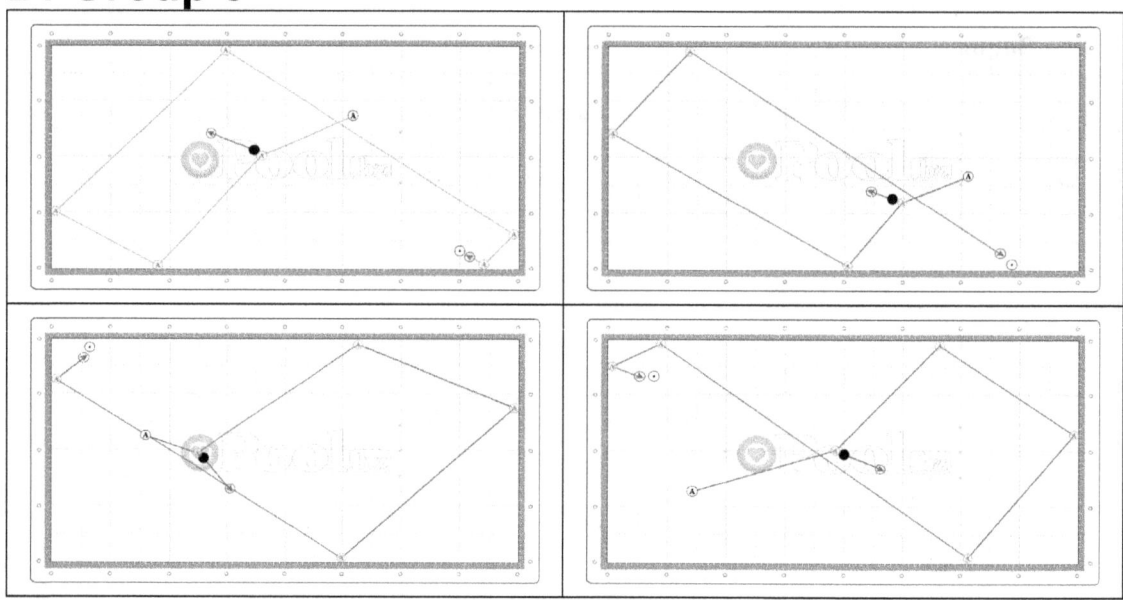

Analysis:

D:8a. _____

D:8b. _____

D:8c. _____

D:8d. _____

D:8a – Setup

Shot Pattern

D:8b – Setup

Shot Pattern

D:8c – Setup

Shot Pattern

D:8d – Setup

Shot Pattern

D: Group 9

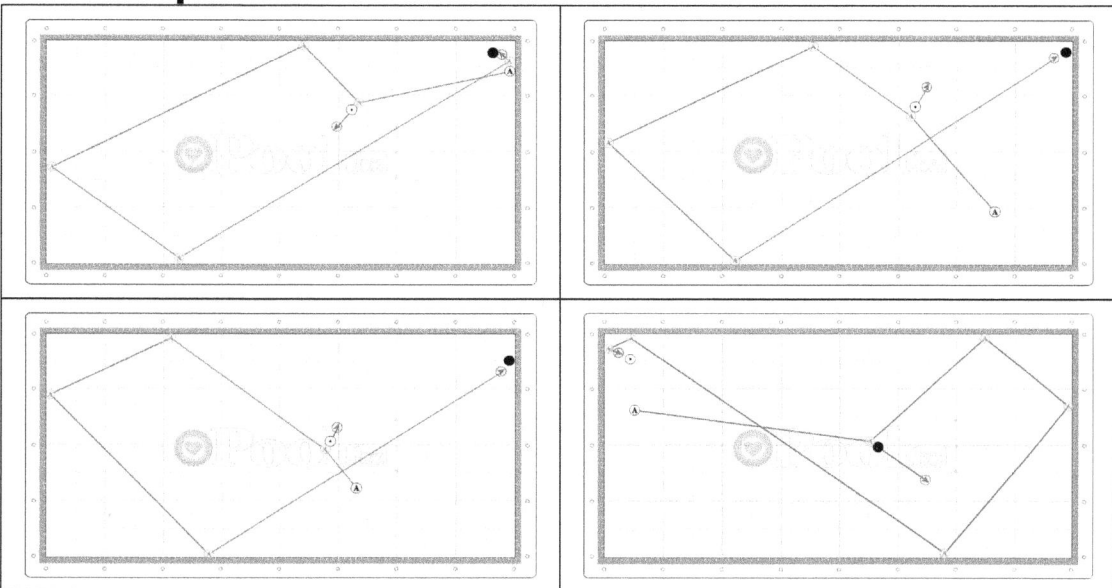

Analysis:

D:9a. _____

D:9b. _____

D:9c. _____

D:9d. _____

D:9a – Setup

Shot Pattern

D:9b – Setup

Shot Pattern

D:9c – Setup

Shot Pattern

D:9d – Setup

Shot Pattern

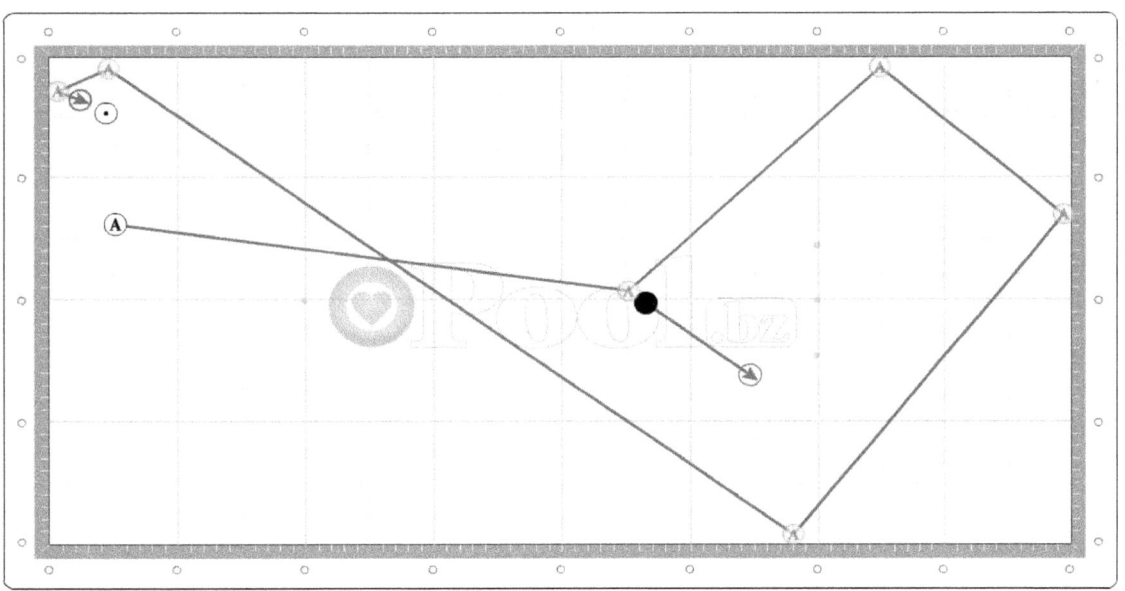

E: Follow into the Corner Pattern

On this series of shots, the CB comes off the first OB and into the next three rails, following the standard "Around the World" pattern. Because the second OB is on the CB's path into the Home corner, the CB contacts the second OB for a score.

E: Group 1

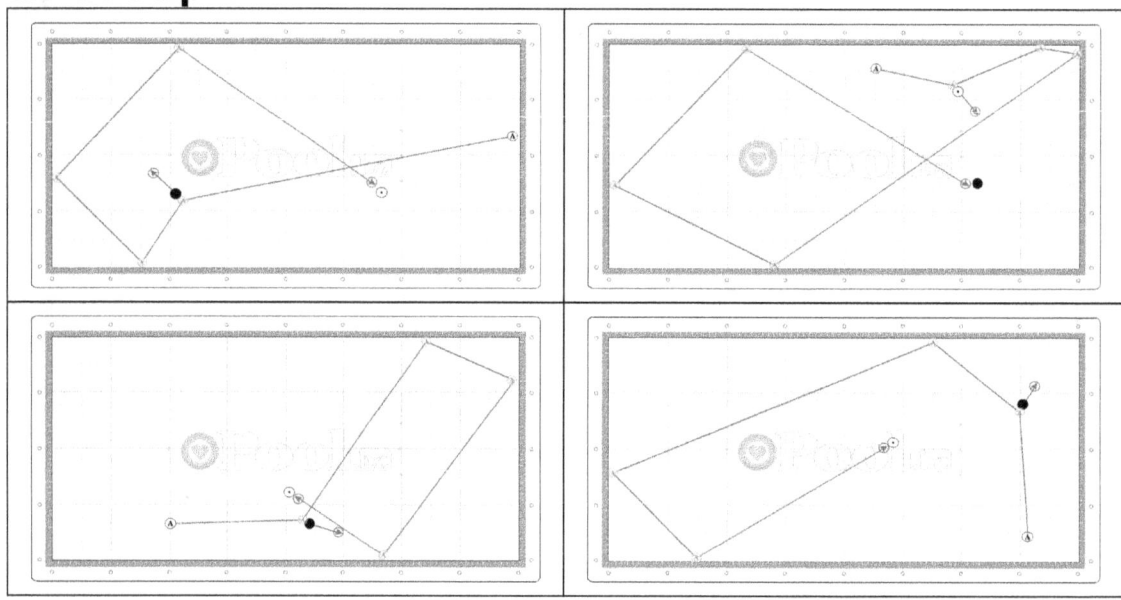

Analysis:

E:1a. _____

E:1b. _____

E:1c. _____

E:1d. _____

E:1a – Setup

Shot Pattern

E:1b – Setup

Shot Pattern

E:1c – Setup

Shot Pattern

E:1d – Setup

Shot Pattern

E: Group 2

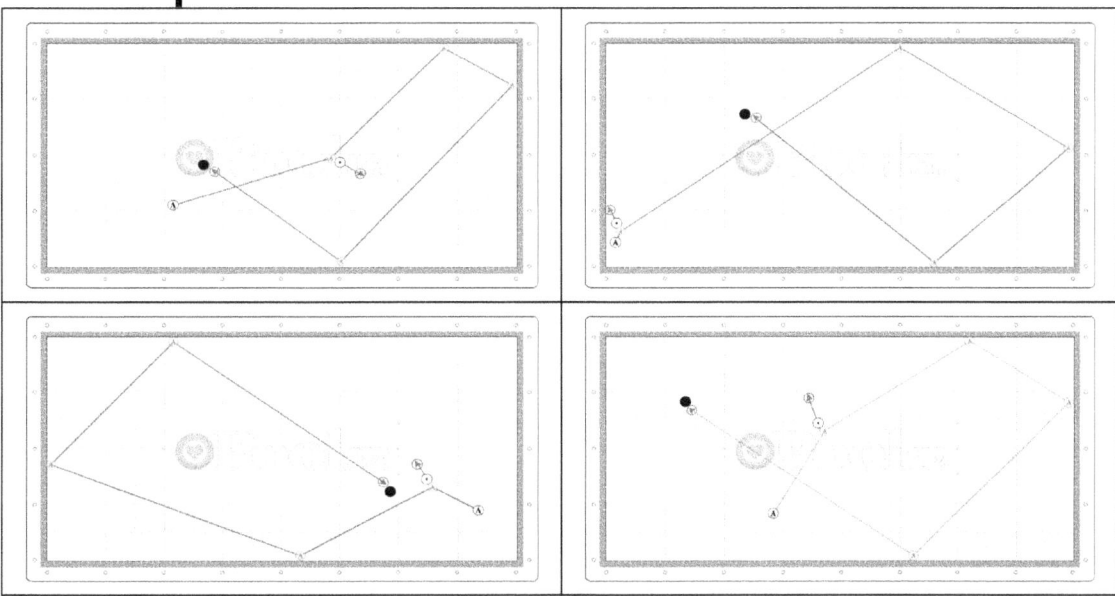

Analysis:

E:2a. _____

E:2b. _____

E:2c. _____

E:2d. _____

E:2a – Setup

Shot Pattern

E:2b – Setup

Shot Pattern

E:2c – Setup

Shot Pattern

E:2d – Setup

Shot Pattern

E: Group 3

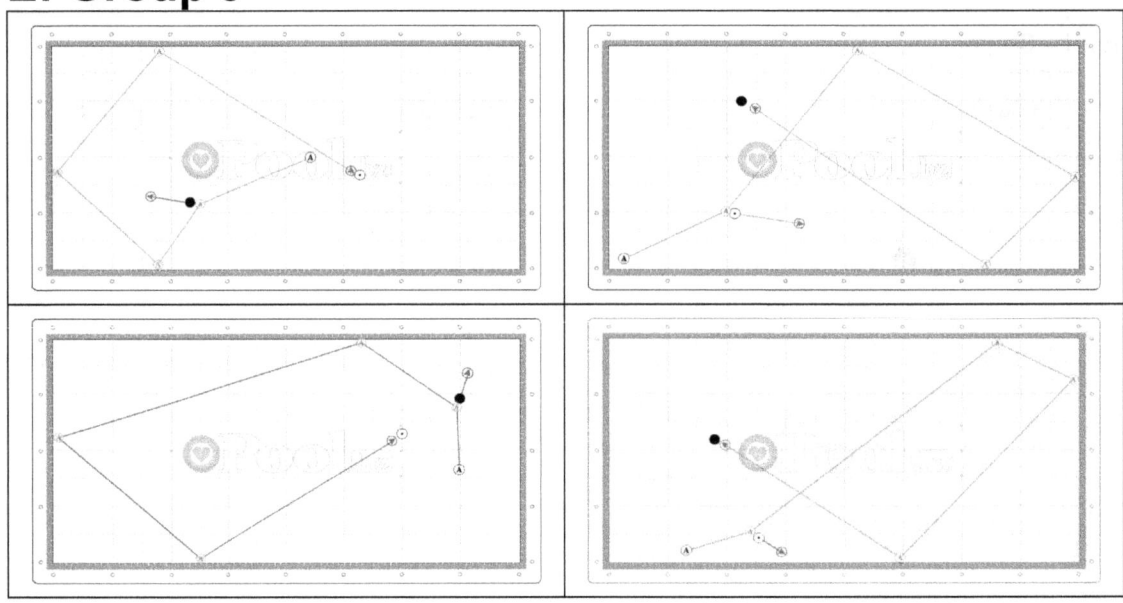

Analysis:

E:3a. _____

E:3b. _____

E:3c. _____

E:3d. _____

E:3a – Setup

Shot Pattern

E:3b – Setup

Shot Pattern

E:3c – Setup

Shot Pattern

E:3d – Setup

Shot Pattern

F: Short Modified Pattern

On these shots, the CB goes into the first OB and into the three rails that follow the standard "Around the World" pattern. However, the pattern is modified, because the second OB is not on the normal path into the Home corner. This means that the shot must be adjusted to bring the CB into the path for a hit on the second OB. On these shots, the pattern is shorter.

F: Group 1

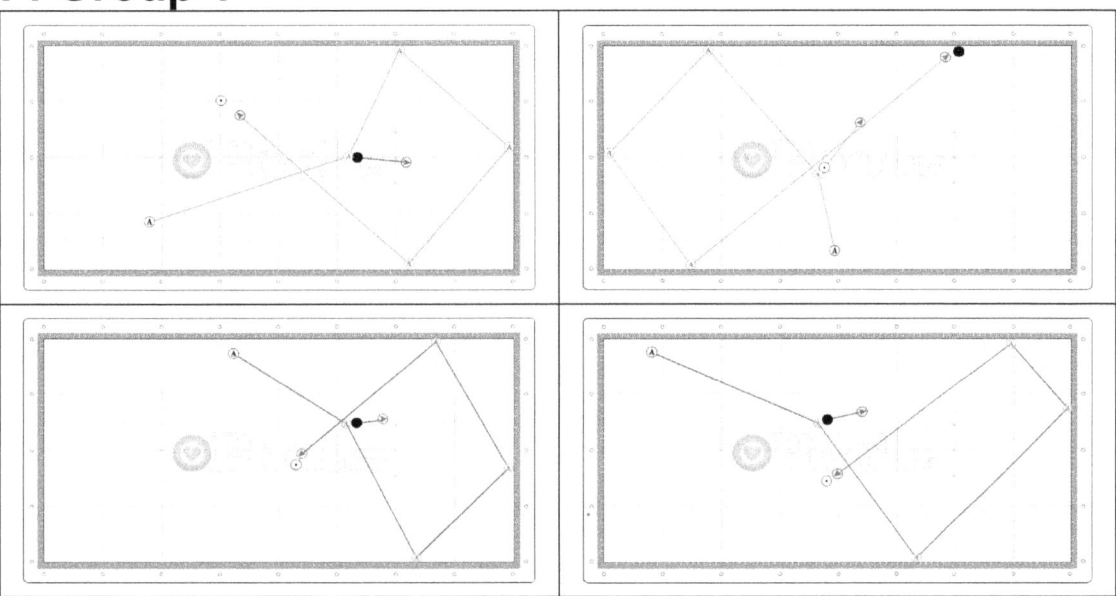

Analysis:

F:1a. _____

F:1b. _____

F:1c. _____

F:1d. _____

F:1a – Setup

Shot Pattern

F:1b – Setup

Shot Pattern

F:1c – Setup

Shot Pattern

F:1d – Setup

Shot Pattern

F: Group 2

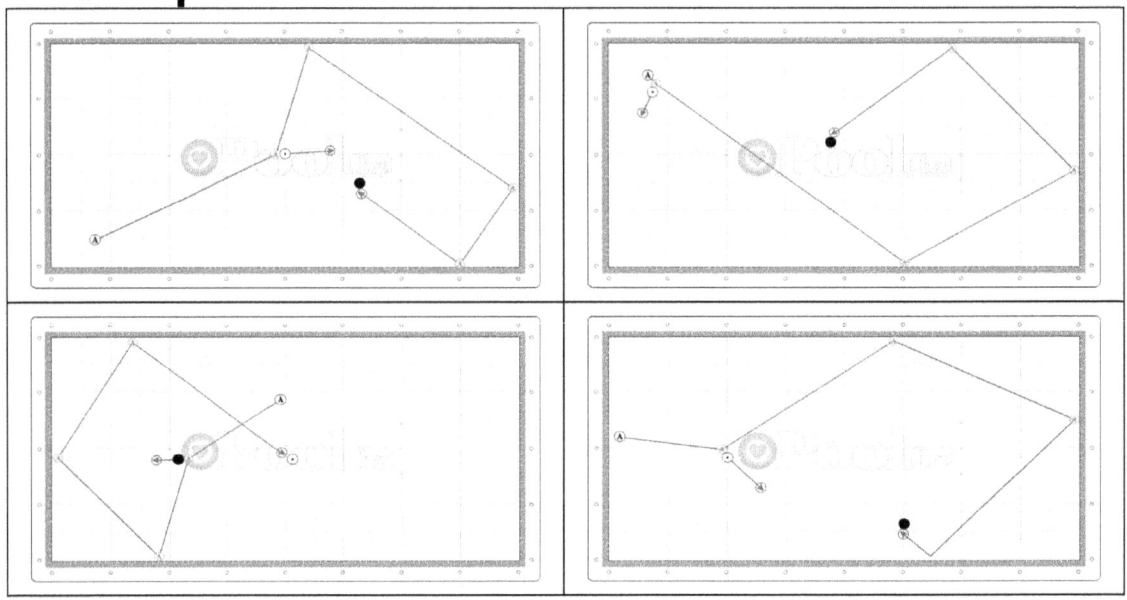

Analysis:

F:2a. _____

F:2b. _____

F:2c. _____

F:2d. _____

F:2a – Setup

Shot Pattern

F:2b – Setup

Shot Pattern

F:2c – Setup

Shot Pattern

F:2d – Setup

Shot Pattern

www.ingramcontent.com/pod-product-compliance
Lightning Source LLC
Chambersburg PA
CBHW080922170426
43201CB00016B/2239